COLOR TES

WICKEDLY
BEAUTIFUL

SHIZ
CHEMISTRY
CLUB

WIZOMANIA

I'M
THROUGH
ACCEPTING
LIMITS
'cause
someone
SAYS
they're so
some
things
I Cannot
CHANGE
but til I try
I'LL NEVER KNOW

ELPHABA

NOT YOUR BASIC
Witch

DEFY GRAVITY

we
can't
all come
and go by
BUBBLE

WICKED

GLINDA

Are people born
WICKED?
Or do they have wickedness
thrust upon them ?

OZMA THE MENDACIOUS
OZMA THE WARRIOR
OZMA THE LIBRARIAN
OZMA THE SCARCELY BELATED

MARVELOUS
MUNCHKINLAND

PINK
goes good with
GREEN

SHIZ
UNIVERSITY

THE
BEST
WITCH
OF ALL

WE·WELCOME·YOU·TO
THE
DEBATABLE
SOCIETY

WELCOME
TO
M
MUNCHKINLAND

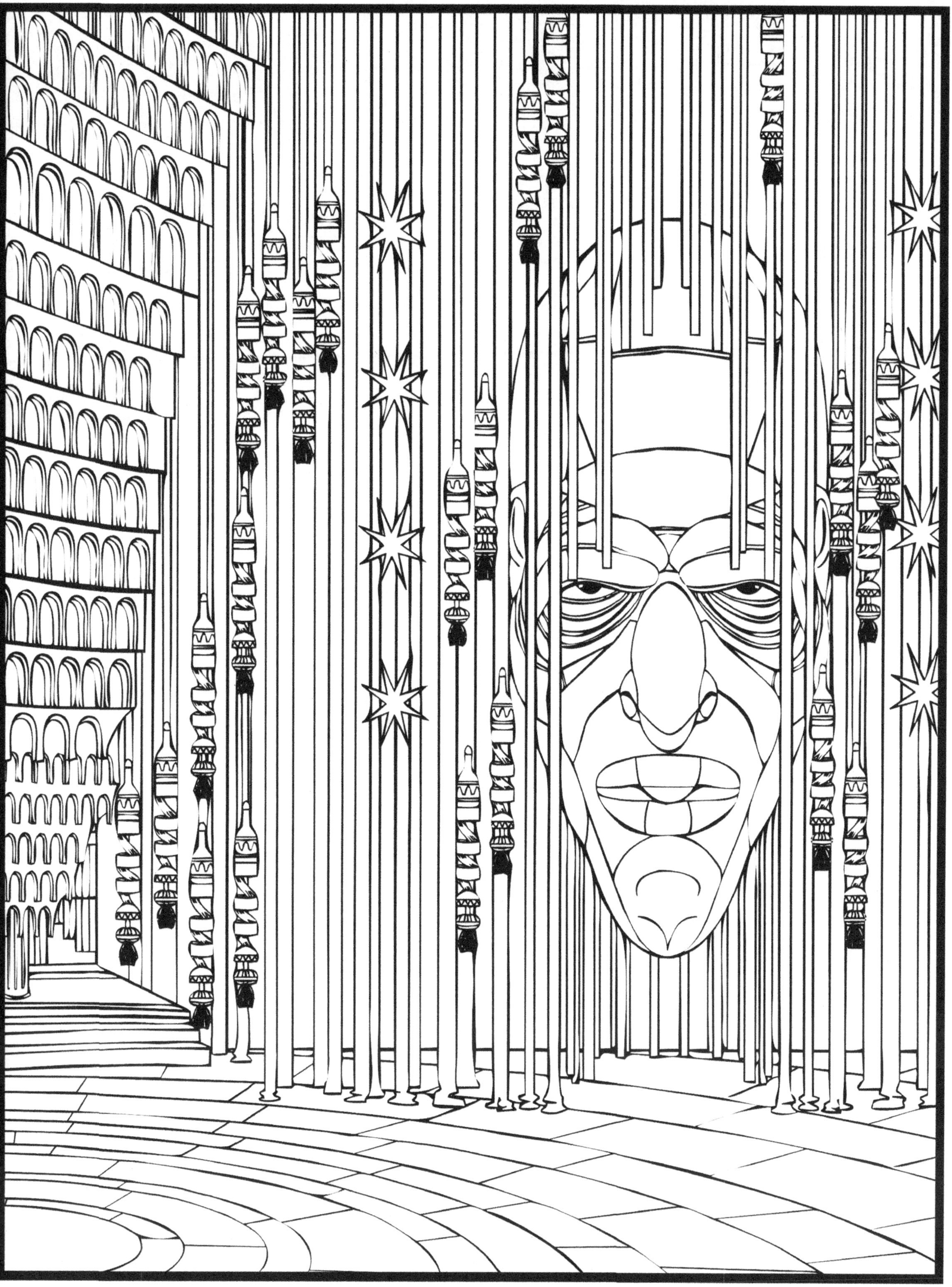

WHO CAN SAY
if I've been
changed
for the
BETTER?
but because
I knew you
I have been changed
FOR
GOOD

A CITY MADE OF
emeralds

EVERYONE
deserves the
CHANCE
TO
fly

IT'S TIME TO
TRUST
MY
Instincts
CLOSE MY
EYES
AND
Leap

IT'S JUST LIFE
SO KEEP
Dancing
THROUGH

YOU'LL BE WITH ME
LIKE A
HANDPRINT
ON MY
HEART

Blank Pages

for drawing, sketching or Writing.

Made in the USA
Las Vegas, NV
15 December 2024

14527952R00063